CW01308640

49 Excuses for Not Eating Your Vegetables

Copyright © 2017, 2022 by James Warwood

Published by Curious Squirrel Press

All rights reserved

No part of this book may be used, stored or reproduced in any manner whatsoever without written permission from the author or publisher.

Book cover design by: James Warwood
Book interior design by: Mala Letra / Lic. Sara F. Salomon

ISBN: 9798439174799
ebook ISBN: B06XQ4XSDD

THE EXCUSE ENCYCLOPEDIA

Book Eight:
49 Excuses for Not Eating Your Vegetables

James Warwood

BOOK EIGHT

Excuses for Not Eating Your Vegetables

VEGETABLE EXCUSES

James Warwood

1. THE DECAYING EXCUSE

Did you know vegetables are perishable? . . .

. . . When cooked, vegetables will decay and go mouldy after 2-3 days. On the other hand, puddings will decay and go mouldy after 5-7 days. So in answer to your statement - *"you can't eat pudding until you've eaten your greens"* - I think I'll wait at the dinner table for the next 4 days and see what happens.

49 Excuses for Not Eating Your Vegetables

2. THE VEG-TABLE EXCUSE

The school nurse has diagnosed me with a severe allergy to veg . . .

VEG ❌   TABLES ❌

. . . Bizarrely, I'm also mildly allergic to tables. Which means that if you ever put vegetables on a table I am sitting at I will die a horrible death. Honestly, it's quite a lethal combination!

James Warwood

3. THE FRUIT & VEG EXCUSE

Did you know that potatos are actually *root vegetables*? . . .

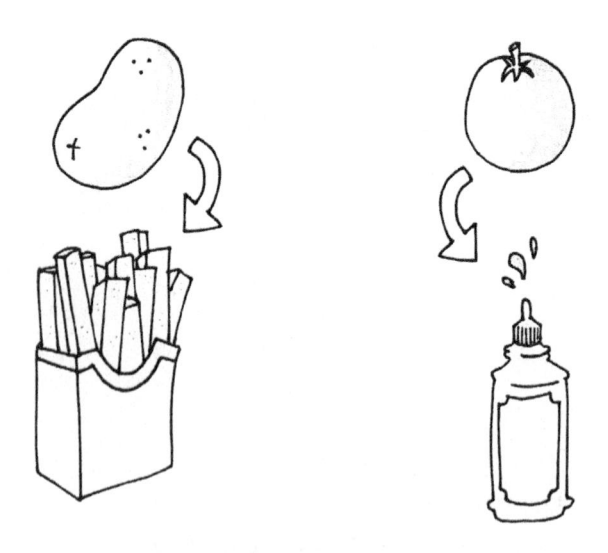

. . . And tomatos are actually *fruit*. So from now on I recommend you serve chips and tomato sauce with every single meal, so that I am always eating my fruit and vegetables.

4. THE HAMSTER EXCUSE

I've been inspired by Hammy my pet Hamster . . .

. . . I'm going to store my vegetables in my massive cheeks for later. Now then, please excuse me while I go to the bathroom to powder my nose.

5. THE HUNGRY BIN EXCUSE

Look, the poor little kitchen bin is hungry . . .

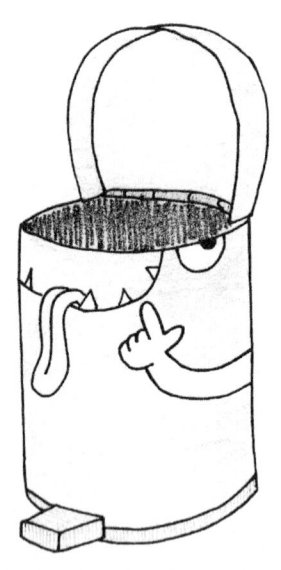

. . . I was going to eat all my yummy sprouts but seeing as I am such a thoughtful young lady I've decided to donate them. Don't worry, kitchen bin, I'll never let you go hungry again.

6. THE MOUSTACHE EXCUSE

Have you heard of Movember? . . .

. . . Men all over the world grow a moustache to raise awareness for Men's Health and I've joined them. Unfortunately I will not be able to squeeze vegetables through my magnificent moustache for a whole month, but it's for a worthy cause.

James Warwood

7. THE LOCK JAW EXCUSE

Em fmm shmmm phm! . . . .

. . . Shmmm chmm brm thmmy wm qumm glm.

49 Excuses for Not Eating Your Vegetables

8. THE TASTE BUDS EXCUSE

Look, here is my tongue map . . .

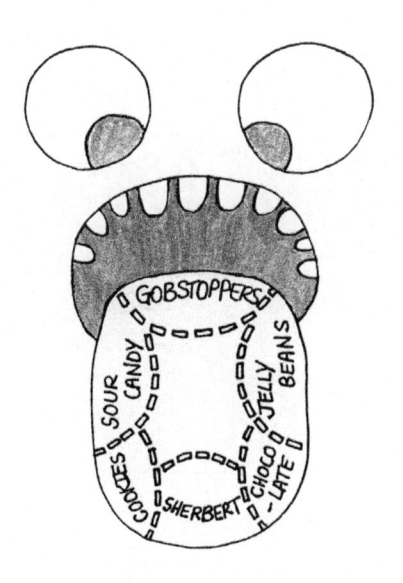

. . . As you can clearly see, my adolescent tongue has not yet developed the taste buds to fully appreciate the complex flavours of vegetables.

James Warwood

9. THE AFRICA EXCUSE

I saw an advert on the TV yesterday . . .

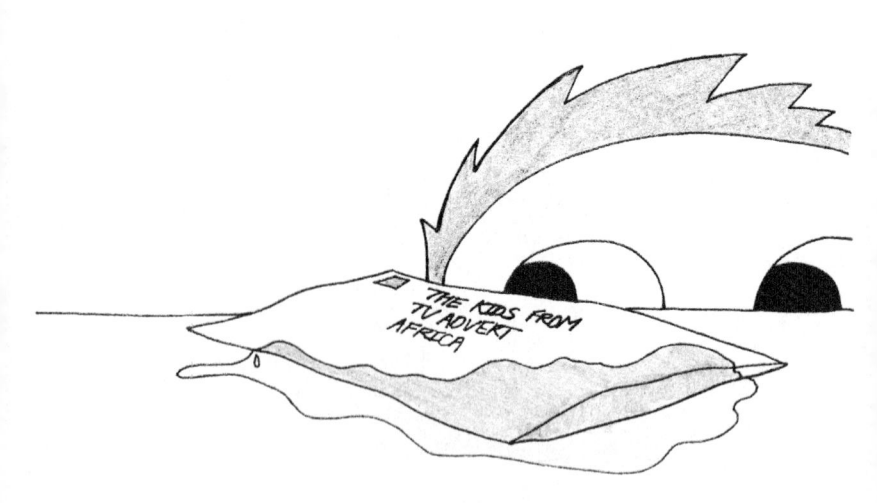

. . . Did you know there are millions of children in Africa going to bed hungry every single day? So, out of the kindness of my heart, I've decided to make a charitable donation.

49 Excuses for Not Eating Your Vegetables

10. THE MULTI-STOMACH EXCUSE

I've done extensive research into the digestive system of children . . .

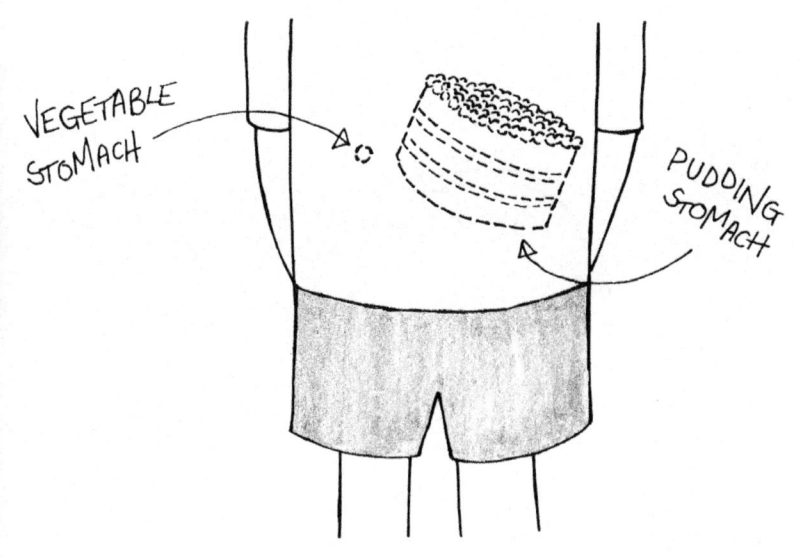

VEGETABLE STOMACH

PUDDING STOMACH

. . . I have discovered something that will change dinner time forever. Children under the age of *[insert your age, plus a few years, here]* have two stomachs: one for vegetables the size of a garden pea, the other for pudding the size of a large chocolate cake.

James Warwood

11. THE PUDDITARIAN EXCUSE

You know Auntie Rebecca? . . .

. . . She is a vegetarian. I've been doing a lot of thinking and she has inspired me to become a *pudditarian*. So from now on I only eat puddings.

49 Excuses for Not Eating Your Vegetables

12. THE NEGOTIATIONS EXCUSE

Sure, I'll eat my vegetables . . .

. . . If you do one of the following things for me: burn down my school, transform my rabbit into a T-Rex, or move the orbit of the earth in a single jump.

13. THE REWARD CHART EXCUSE

You know how I really struggle to eat my vegetables . . .

VEGETABLE REWARD CHART	
Days eating his veggies	The Reward
1	Trip to Disneyland
2	Trip to the Moon
3	One-way trip to the centre of the Earth (for my big sister)

. . . Well I decided to make a reward chart to help me. I'll need you to sign the bottom, as it's a legally binding contract.

49 Excuses for Not Eating Your Vegetables

14. THE MUSICAL EXCUSE

Scientists think that music makes food taste better...

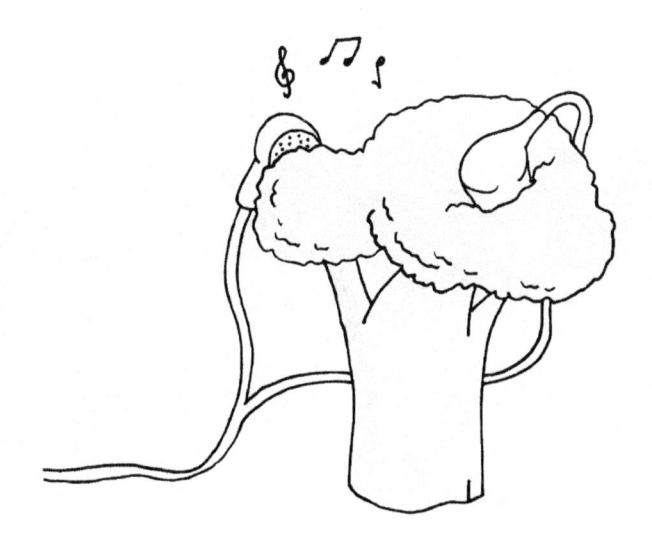

...Seeing as this piece of broccoli tastes absolutely disgusting I've made an eight hour long playlist for it to listen to.

15. THE DINNER WITCH EXCUSE

I've got to leave all my vegetables tonight . . .

THE DINNER WITCH

. . . On *[insert date here]* every year the Dinner Witch visits and if you don't leave her vegetable offerings she will turn you into an ugly little toad with an embarrassing haircut.

16. THE PIZZA EXCUSE

Behold! The only food I need to eat for the rest of my life . . .

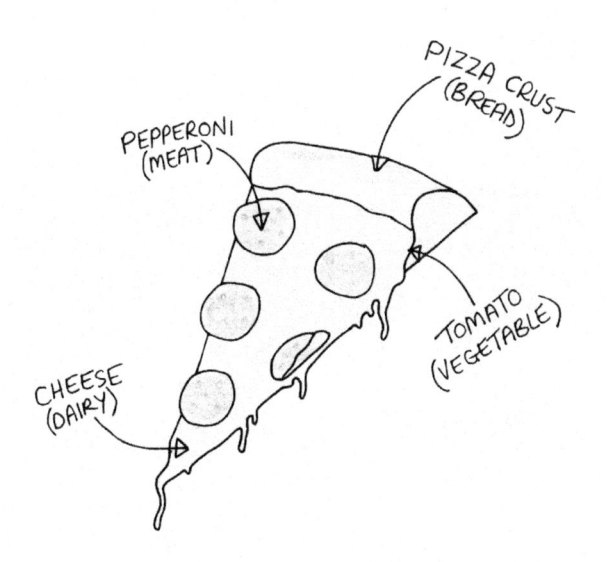

PIZZA CRUST (BREAD)
PEPPERONI (MEAT)
TOMATO (VEGETABLE)
CHEESE (DAIRY)

. . . PIZZA! This magical wonder food contains every food group, including vegetables. It's a nutritional and healthy slice of pure happiness.

James Warwood

17. THE CATAPULT EXCUSE

I've invented a new, ground-breaking method of feeding yourself...

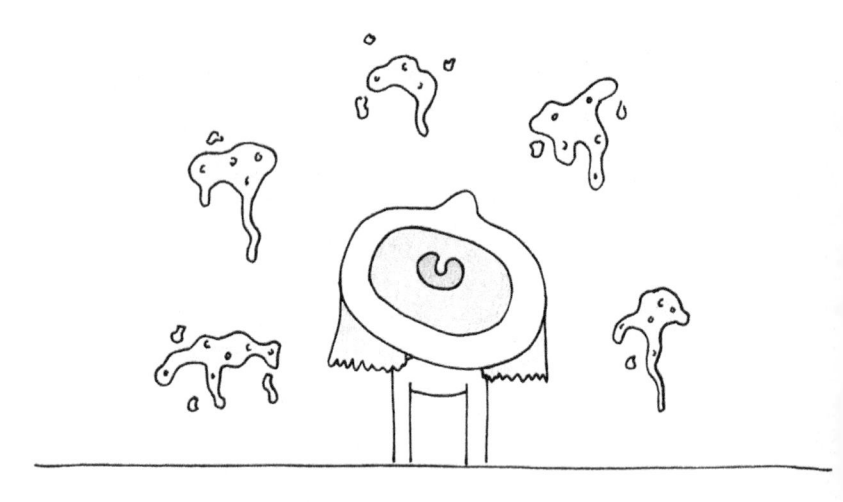

...I call it – *The Vegetable Catapult*. Admittedly my new invention is still in the testing phase. I'll make some minor adjustments and commence the 2nd round of testing at dinner tomorrow.

49 Excuses for Not Eating Your Vegetables

18. THE DISTRACTION EXCUSE

Right, I'm going to eat my vegetables now. Are you ready? . . .

...WOOOOOOOOOOOOOOOOOOOOOOW, WHAT IS THAT IN THE WINDOW BEHIND YOU!?! Did you not see that? I can't believe you missed it. On the bright side, I did manage to eat all my vegetables.

19. THE OPEN DOOR EXCUSE

Oh no, did you leave the front door open? . . .

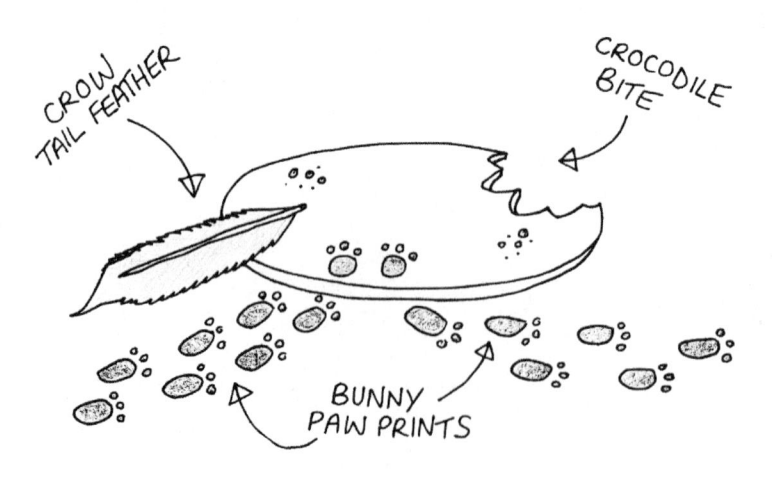

. . . Wild animals have stolen my precious vegetables. A crow stole my peas and a rabbit stole my carrots. Did you know that an alligator's favourite food is Brussels sprouts? Well, you do now.

20. THE ALL-IN-ONE PILL EXCUSE

Behold! The All-In-One Pill . . .

...It contains everything the human body needs in one tiny capsule. So I don't need to eat my vegetables anymore. I know it looks like a Tic-Tac and tastes like a Tic-Tac, but I assure you, it is not a Tic-Tac.

James Warwood

21. THE BLENDER DIET EXCUSE

I've decided to go on the *Blender Diet*...

... From now on I require all my vegetables to be blended into a smoothie. According to Dr. Snozzcumber, the food scientist behind the *Blender Diet*, they should also be mixed with two scoops of vanilla ice cream, three meringue nests and six tablespoons of sugar.

49 Excuses for Not Eating Your Vegetables

22. THE BRACES EXCUSE

I'm back from the dentist, she said to read you this letter . . .

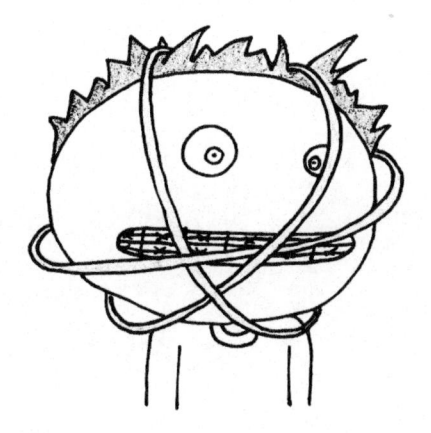

. . . [Open fake letter and read aloud]

Dear Parents. I am writing to inform you that the braces your son has been fitted with have an unfortunate manufacturing fault. If healthy food comes into contact with the braces it they will dissolve and all his teeth will fall out. P.S. I recommend feeding him fries covered in tomato ketchup and fizzy pop.

23. THE OBSTACLE COURSE EXCUSE

Fine, I'll open wide for the airplane to land . . .

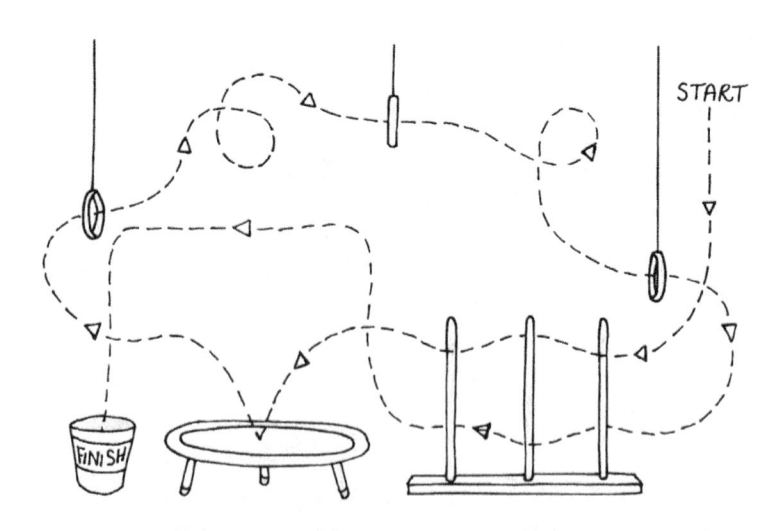

. . . But only if the pilot is able to complete this obstacle course. I do hope the vegetable pilot has a seatbelt on that plane of his.

49 Excuses for Not Eating Your Vegetables

24. THE SUPERSTARS EXCUSE

Hang on, I recognise these guys . . .

. . . OMG! They're film stars. The tomato is called Bob, the cucumber is called Larry and this little one is called Junior Asparagus. I can't eat them!

25. THE SCALES EXCUSE

Good News! I've been cast as Oliver in our school production of Oliver Twist . . .

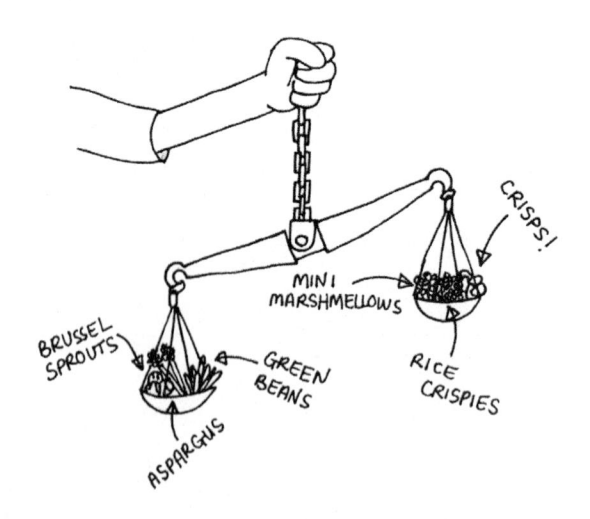

. . . It's a soprano part, so I will have to sing very high notes. My Drama Teacher has given me a strict diet of light and airy foods to keep my vocal chords healthy. No heavy vegetables for me.

49 Excuses for Not Eating Your Vegetables

26. THE SNAIL POLICE EXCUSE

A snail has stolen my cabbage . . .

. . . Don't worry. I've called the Snail Police and they're already giving chase to the perpetrator. Should have my cabbage back in 3-5 days.

James Warwood

27. THE DIRTY HANDS EXCUSE

I was going to eat my vegetables but my hands were dirty . . .

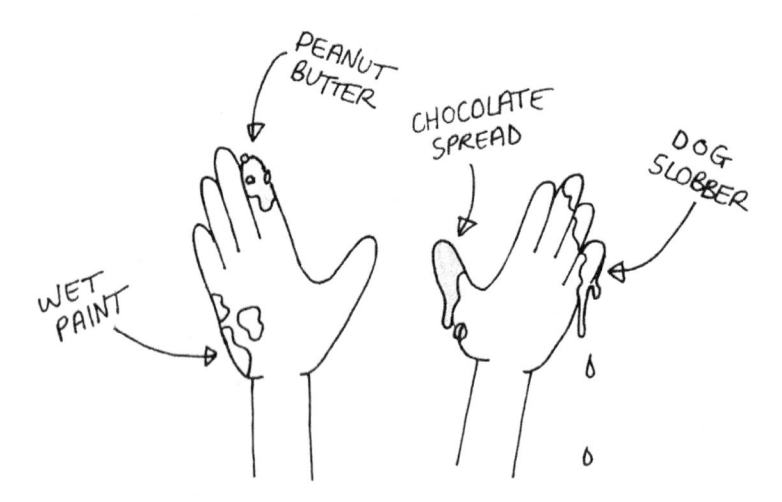

PEANUT BUTTER
CHOCOLATE SPREAD
DOG SLOBBER
WET PAINT

. . . So I washed my hands but then slipped and touched wet paint. I washed them again only for the dog to lick them. Then finally I washed them for a third time only to accidentally put my hands in jars of chocolate spread and peanut butter. Silly me!

49 Excuses for Not Eating Your Vegetables

28. THE CARROT VISION EXCUSE

My science experiment has gone slightly wrong . . .

. . . I ate twenty carrots at school, to test the *Carrots Help you See in the Dark* theory. Now everything is orange and I have a strange desire to burrow a hole and thump my left foot.

James Warwood

29. THE GENETICS EXCUSE

Back from the kitchen already? . . .

. . . While you were gone I successfully genetically modified this parsnip into the shape of a chocolate bar. I will now eat my vegetables, and I shall do so with considerable pleasure.

30. THE CAULIFLOWER EXCUSE

Look! Look what's happened to my hair . . .

. . . I told you I've eaten too much cauliflower. Now look at my hair, it's turned into a cauliflower. I need you to buy as much cheese as you can, melt it all in a big pot and slowly dip my hair in.

James Warwood

31. THE VEGGIE COMA EXCUSE

[Leave this letter at the end of your bed] . . .

... *Dear* [insert name here] *Parents, I've got some bad news. Your daughter has slipped into a vegetable coma. She has eaten too many vegetables. I recommend you spoon feed her chocolate spread until she wakes up. Yours sincerely, the Family Doctor.*

32. THE HAUNTED EXCUSE

Don't go down the vegetable aisle!

. . .

. . . It's been closed by the Paranormal Police. I read somewhere that the aisle is haunted by a poltergeist called Jack the Tripper. He trips people up while browsing for tomatoes.

33. THE COOKING INSTRUCTIONS EXCUSE

Do you smell something burning? . .

. . . Oh dear, you mean you're not meant to spit-roast vegetables on an open fire for twenty hours?

49 Excuses for Not Eating Your Vegetables

34. THE MAIL ORDER VEG EXCUSE

I decided to order our vegetables online . . .

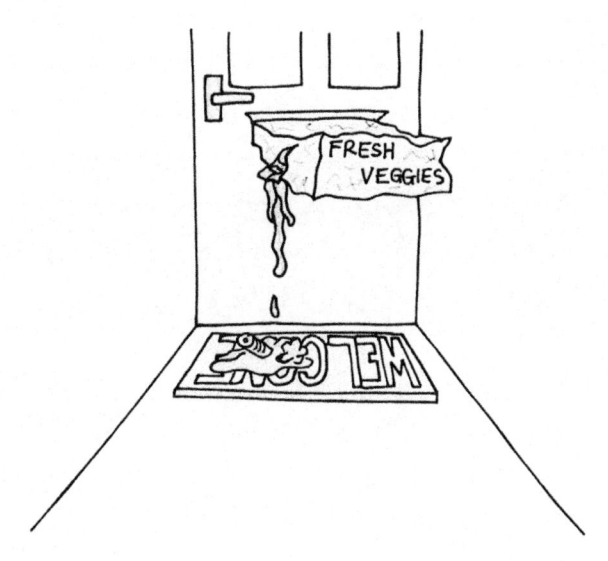

. . . They call it Mail Order Veg. I think it is a fantastic idea. Unfortunately our letter box doesn't agree, and neither does the postman who decided to force the parcel through.

James Warwood

35. THE VIRTUAL REALITY EXCUSE

But I am eating my vegetables . . .

. . . This virtual reality headset is very realistic. My virtual broccoli is a little on the chewy side, but very tasty.

49 Excuses for Not Eating Your Vegetables

36. THE ART PROJECT EXCUSE

This week's homework is to make vegetable art...

... Look at my beautiful creations. I've made an octopus from my banana, a mouse from my pear and a blue whale from my cucumber.

James Warwood

37. THE VEG CLASS EXCUSE

Thanks for the veggies but I've already had my five-a-day . . .

FULL OF VEGETABLES

. . . There's a new lesson at school called *Veg Class*. We learned about the wonders of vegetables and ate loads of different types. This week's homework is to eat our twenty-a-week, which refers to eating a healthy variety of sweets and chocolate throughout the week.

49 Excuses for Not Eating Your Vegetables

38. THE DRUNK DRIVER EXCUSE

Stop right there! . . .

. . . I'm the Train Driver Inspector and I have reason to believe that the driver of this train is drunk at the controls. There was an anonymous tip off that this carrot has been marinating in red wine all night.

James Warwood

39. THE PESTICIDES EXCUSE

I can't eat this carrot . . .

. . . There are pesticides all over it. Yuck! Don't worry, I'll make sure it is disposed of in a safe and humane way.

40. THE MYTH EXCUSE

Do carrots really glow in the dark?

. . .

. . . Oh sorry, I got it the wrong way around. *Eating* carrots helps you see in the dark. I'm going to need three plasters and an ice pack please.

James Warwood

41. THE MAGIC EXCUSE

Watch the Brussels sprout . . .

. . . Tadaaaaaaa! The Brussels sprout has gone. Now I'll make the rest of my vegetables disappear too. Good boy, Fido.

49 Excuses for Not Eating Your Vegetables

42. THE BACTERIA EXCUSE

In today's Science lesson we studied bacteria...

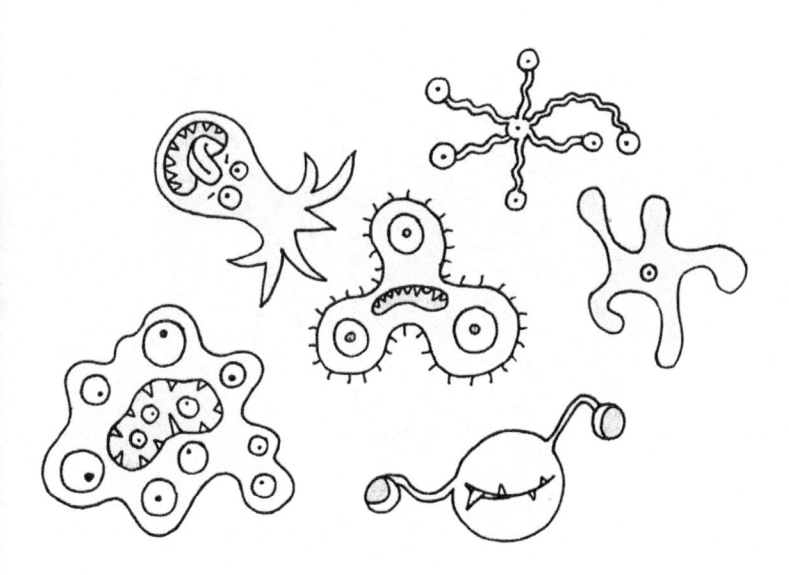

... Did you know there is good and bad bacteria? Don't worry, I've checked which kind of bacteria is on my plate of vegetables and can tell you it's all the bad kind.

James Warwood

43. THE TASTE TESTER EXCUSE

Fido is a very good boy . . .

. . . He is my new food tester. He checks that my vegetables are not poisonous. Looks to me like today's vegetables were non-toxic, and I can tell by the way Fido is licking his lips that they were tasty too.

49 Excuses for Not Eating Your Vegetables

44. THE SETTING THE TABLE EXCUSE

Look, I set the table all by myself . . .

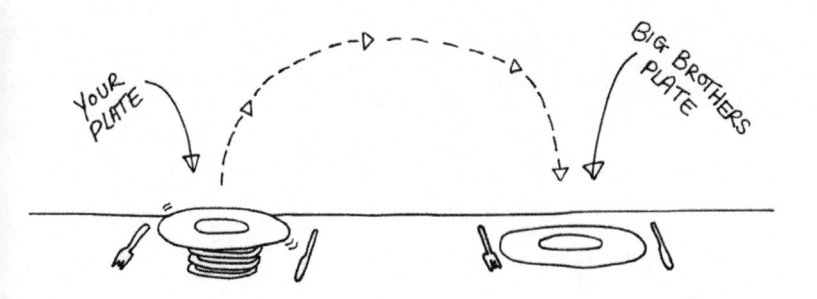

YOUR PLATE

BIG BROTHERS PLATE

. . . I will be sitting on the left and my big brother will be sitting on the right. As you can see, my dinner plate is ready for my vegetables.

James Warwood

45. THE BIB EXCUSE

I know that I'm a bit old for a bib now . . .

. . . It's just a precaution. I don't want any of my yummy vegetables to be wasted by falling on the floor.

49 Excuses for Not Eating Your Vegetables

46. THE GREEN EXCUSE

Oh, I almost forgot to tell you. I'm allergic to the colour green . . .

. . . I can no longer wear my Hulk fancy dress costume, use green felt tip pens or eat any green vegetables. I'm going to miss broccoli, and colouring in the bottom bits of flowers, and also hulk smashing stuff.

James Warwood

47. THE NUTRITION EXCUSE

I've developed a new, groundbreaking eating technique...

...With the help of these state-of-the-art nutrition glasses I can soak up nutrients *with my mind*. Unfortunately the glasses only work on vegetables, so I still have to eat chocolate the traditional way.

49 Excuses for Not Eating Your Vegetables

48. THE GARDENER EXCUSE

Good news. I've become a vegetable gardener . . .

. . . I've started by burying all the vegetables that were on my plate in my new vegetable plot. In a years time we'll all have plenty of vegetables to eat. I do hope you're feeling patient.

James Warwood

49. THE 30,000 EXCUSE

As a child I am a 'Supertaster' [this is true, you are a supertaster]...

30,000 TASTE BUDS

10,000 TASTE BUDS

A FEW VEGETABLES (EVERY NOW AND THEN)

LOTS AND LOTS OF VEGETABLES!

...I was born with around 30,000 taste buds [true] which means eating bitter vegetables is a very intense experience and can be extremely difficult [again, true]. I'll continue to try and eat my vegetables, as I know they are good for me. And remember, once I'm an adult I'll have around 10,000 taste buds left and will probably love them [and, believe it or not, you probably will].

49 Excuses for Not Eating Your Vegetables

BONUS: ULCER EXCUSE

I can't eat my vegetables today. I have an ulcer . . .

. . . Peas and sweetcorn are not going to help. The one and only cure is Neapolitan Ice Cream.

James Warwood

BONUS: BALANCED DIET EXCUSE

Remember what you said about eating a balanced diet? . . .

. . . Well, these vegetables are rubbish at balancing, so clearly I can't eat them.

49 Excuses for Not Eating Your Vegetables

BONUS: CARROT CAKE EXCUSE

I have a big announcement . . .

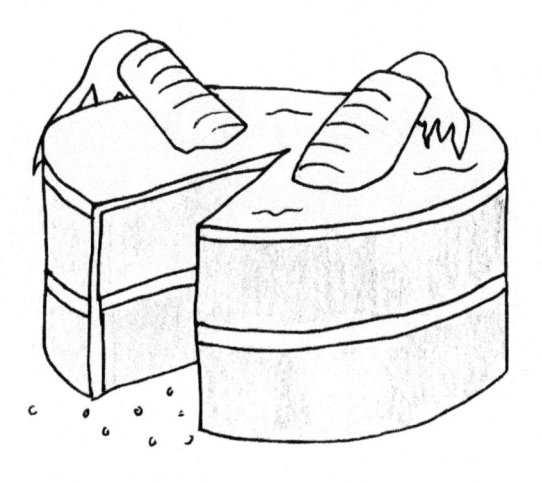

. . . From now on I only eat vegetables that have been baked into cakes. Apparently, carrot cake is very tasty so let's have that for dinner tonight.

BONUS: CRIME SCENE EXCUSE

By the way, the police just called . . .

. . . They've informed me that my dinner plate was the scene of a terrible crime. It's been cornered off to preserve the crime scene.

49 Excuses for Not Eating Your Vegetables

BONUS: CARNIVORE EXCUSE

I learnt in science today that I am a carnivore . . .

. . . That means I can only eat meat. My little sister on the other hand is definitely a herbivore, so she can have all of my vegetables from now on.

James Warwood

BONUS: VEG BEARER EXCUSE

Good news! I have hired a Veg Bearer...

... This dog will be tasting all my vegetables before I eat them from now on. So far, I haven't been able to eat any of my vegetables as he's very keen to be called a *good boy*.

49 Excuses for Not Eating Your Vegetables

BONUS: HEALTHY BIN EXCUSE

Have you noticed our bin is getting a belly? . . .

BIN BELLY

. . . I've started a campaign to help our kitchen bin eat healthier. From now on I'm going to throw all of my veggies in the bin and make sure it does twenty sit ups every day.

James Warwood

BONUS: VEG POWER EXCUSE

I can't eat my vegetables tonight...

... I'm working on new renewable power sources. Pass me your iPhone and I'll charge it up to full power with my veggie power.

49 Excuses for Not Eating Your Vegetables

BONUS: CANNIBAL EXCUSE

Erm, well, you see . . . I'm a Brussels sprout . . .

. . . Therefore, I can't eat them. One of them could be my long-lost relative.

James Warwood

BONUS: TONGUE-ACHE EXCUSE

You've heard about toothache, right? . . .

. . . Well, I've got a tongueache. Quick, get me every single flavour of ice cream ever invented and the biggest duvet in the world, QUICK!!!

BONUS: RAW VEG EXCUSE

I read a very interesting article online today . . .

. . . It said that eating raw vegetables is much healthier than eating cooked vegetables. So, if you eat this raw Brussels sprout than I'll eat my veggies.

James Warwood

BONUS: FUSSY PARASITE EXCUSE

I have a lovely parasite (called Steve) living in my belly . . .

I ONLY LIKE CAKE

. . . Bad news is that Steve hates vegetables. I'm trying to be a polite host, just like you taught me, so please serve me two slices of Chocolate Cake for dinner tonight. One slice for Steve and one slice for me.

ABOUT THE AUTHOR

James Warwood is a writer and illustrator who lives on the borders of North Wales with his wife, two sons, and cactus (called Steve the Cactus).

He has a degree in Theology, which at the time seemed like a great idea, until he released he didn't want to become an RE Teacher. Instead, he writes laugh-out-loud middle grade fiction and non-fiction. He also fills them with his silly cartoons. He is the bestselling author of the EXCUSE ENCYCLOPEDIA and the TRUTH OR POOP SERIES.

James likes whiskey, squirrels, reading silly books, playing his bass guitar, and Greggs Sausage Rolls. He does not like losing at board games or having to writing about himself in the third person.

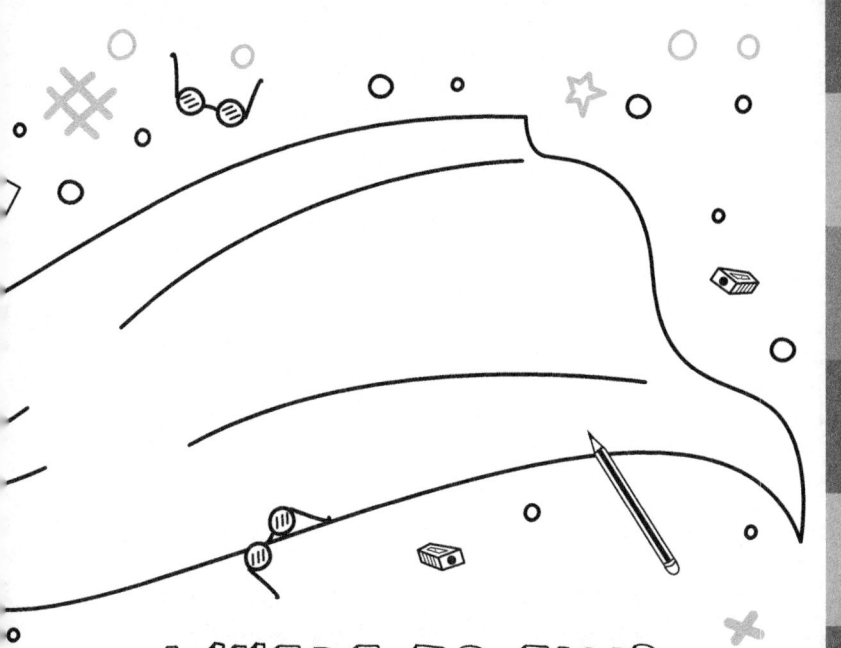

WHERE TO FIND JAMES ONLINE

Website: www.cjwarwood.com
Goodreads: James Warwood
Instagram: CJWarwood
Facebook: James Warwood

Want to join the
BOOKS & BISCUITS
CLUB?

Scan me to sign up
to the newsletter.

SO, WHAT'S NEXT?

MIDDLE-GRADE STAND-ALONE FICTION

The Chef Who Cooked Up a Catastrophe
The Boy Who Stole One Million Socks
The Girl Who Vanquished the Dragon

TRUTH OR POOP SERIES

True or false quiz books.
Learn something new and laugh as you do it!

THE EXCUSE ENCYCLOPEDIA

11 more books to read!

GET THEM ALL IN THIS 12 IN 1 BUMPER EDITION!

820-page compendium of knowledge with 180 BONUS excuses

Scan me to activate your

25% DISCOUNT

Printed in Great Britain
by Amazon